New York
Living Rooms

Dominique
Nabokov

New York
Living Rooms

Dominique
Nabokov

The Overlook Press

First published in 1998 by
The Overlook Press, Peter Mayer Publishers, Inc.
Lewis Hollow Road
Woodstock, New York 12498

Introduction copyright © 1998 James Fenton
Photographs copyright © 1998 Dominique Nabokov

Excerpt from "The Common Life" from W.H. AUDEN: COLLECTED POEMS by W.H. Auden, edited
by Edward Mendelson. Copyright © 1963 by W.H. Auden. Reprinted by permission of
Random House, Inc.

Library of Congress Cataloging-in-Publications Data

Nabokov, Dominique.
   New York living rooms / Dominique Nabokov : introduction by James Fenton
        p.   cm.
   ISBN 0-87951-875-8
   1. Living rooms—New York (State)—New York—Pictorial works.
   2. Interior decoration—New York (State)—New York—Pictorial works.
   3. Celebrities—Homes and haunts—New York (State)—New York—Pictorial works.
   I. Title.
   NK2117.L5N23   1998
   747.7'5'097471—dc21   98-16619
        747·75 NAB   CIP

Manufactured in the United States of America

ISBN 0-87951-875-8

First Edition.

9 8 7 6 5 4 3 2 1

acknowledgments

I am indebted to Tina Brown, David Kuhn and Crary Pullen of *The New Yorker* of 1995 who started me on this project, also to the photographer Pascal Prince for introducing me to Polaroid Colorgraph type 691 film.

I am also grateful to Peter Mayer, Tracy Carns and Hermann Lademann of The Overlook Press for making *New York Living Rooms* possible. I'd like to thank all the people in *New York Living Rooms* for letting me in. And last but not least, Barbara Epstein of *The New York Review of Books* for encouraging me in this New York project.

preface

New York Living Rooms is not exactly about interior decoration. Although it represents a special stylistic and aesthetic approach, it is above all a document. No rearranging, no adding of bouquets, no use of flood lights. I approach the living rooms like I approach the people I photograph: a portrait as close to reality as possible.

I have always been an advocate of photography free of heavy equipment; if I can avoid strobe, flash, and even a tripod, I do. I believe in mobility. For this book I used the Polaroid camera 600 SE, this time with a tripod and the Polaroid Colorgraph type 691 film, which provides a full color positive transparency in 4 minutes (exactly the time it takes to boil my eggs)—what a thrill and relief it is to have the result right away! Color photography is rarely a satisfying medium—too beautiful or too ugly, and mostly banal. With this particular film I like the accidental, eccentric colors. The color tones do not alter the impact of the image.

This lightweight, unobtrusive, and fast approach to shooting, with its accidental and immediate results, gave me the wonderful feeling of being a sleuth-voyeur. I could easily go on and on, opening the doors of New York City for years—what fun! Unfortunately it seems impossible: this film has been discontinued.

Dominique Nabokov
New York June 17, 1998

introduction

by

James Fenton

"A room is too small, (said Auden, he was talking about living rooms)
if its occupants cannot forget at will
that they are not alone, too big
if it gives them any excuse in a quarrel
for raising their voices."

He was thinking of a living room as a place on which two partners-for-life
impose their common style, a style which confronts the visitor, allowing
him to decide "whether he would like to see more of us." But that is a
harsh assignment for mere decor to undertake, and I could sympathize with
a room that remained resolutely enigmatic. Like the London apartment of
the minimalist architect, broken into by thieves not long ago. The thieves
took nothing, not because there was nothing to take but because - being
unversed in minimalism - they were fooled into thinking they were in an
empty apartment. (None of the drawers had handles, none of the cupboards
had knobs.)

There can come a sort of savage delight from a room with which one has
nothing whatever to do, but which one must occupy for a month or two. In
a service apartment or an apartment hotel, comfortably equipped but in a
style to which one is utterly indifferent, with a kitchen that says "To
be realistic - you'll be eating out most nights," and a living room that
suggests "Here you may receive a guest, without any hint of intimacy. Those
simple assertions of your occupancy - the flowers you bought, the books
you may choose to leave out - have nothing to reveal about where you are
coming from, or what your next destination may be. That bowl of fruit is
just a bowl of fruit. Nothing may be deduced from it."

To invite you into my living room may not be to admit you into "the privacy of my own home." It may well be the best way of keeping you at arm's
length. I lived in a country where the very possession of a spacious living room implied such relative wealth that it soon brought pressures and
responsibilities in its wake. Suitors, petitioners, postulants were the
kind of people one might expect to find in the living room. I remember a

man - the eager brother of an acquaintance - who was just starting out as a dealer in futures. We sat in the living room, under the ceiling fan, and he spread his charts before me, explaining the wealth that must certainly accrue. I listened indifferently. The charts slid around in the breeze. The futures dealer became desperate. Surely to goodness there was somewhere more intimate we could go, somewhere he could explain to me, confide in me, impart the arcana. His eyes searched wildly around the house. He was on the verge of creating a fortune for me - in copper futures - if only he could be admitted to my den, my office or study or wherever these transactions took place. When I told him that whatever he had to say could be said in the living room, it was taken as a brutal rebuff.

What luck to have a living room, where such rebuffs can be administered. What luxury to be able to calibrate exactly the amount of intimacy a living room is to imply. Auden thought of his living room as a place that he might enter without knocking and leave without a bow - but a place of encounter, nevertheless, a place where the I and Thou of a partnership may create a common space. One might wonder, though, whether the rooms shown in these photographs are always that kind of intimate meeting-ground, or whether the public function of the living room is not more in evidence: this is where we entertain, this is as far as you will get.

The photographer has not barged in unannounced. Most of the rooms have been tidied, or have anyway been kept tidy. But they have not been given a tweak by any stylist - and in this respect the photographs differ from the celebrity interior genre. The photographer seems not to be a satirist. Had she been seeking the absurd or the grotesque she could have come up with a quite different list. On the other hand, she is not unamused either, to have built up this dossier on the types of display in which the owners of living rooms of this kind will indulge.

The owners are absent. We do not want them interfering with our intrusion of their. . . privacy? Is this living room private, or is it domesticity's public face? Does living take place here, or is this room the equivalent of those false chambers in Egyptian tombs, created to fool the thieves? Does this style proceed from the taste of the owners, or was it ordered over the phone? Was it haggled over, fussed over, arrived at by degrees? Or did someone say: help me out, I need a style to hide behind. As one might say: give me a passport, a driver's license, a new name, an identity. Give me a living room where I can survive undetected. Give me a pedigree, background, taste.

Tom Sachs, artist, Little Italy

John "Lypsinka" Epperson, drag performer, The Garment District

Nan Goldin, photographer, Greenwich Village

Geoffrey Firth, hair stylist, Upper East Side

Susan Molinari, former U.S. representative, Staten Island

Darryl Turner, photographer, Chelsea

Ned Rorem, composer, Central Park West

Susan Minot, writer, Greenwich Village

Jerome Robbins, director, choreographer, Upper East Side

Tim Lovejoy, artist, Park Avenue

Leo Lerman, writer, and Gray Foy, editor, The Osborne

Quentin Crisp, writer, East Village

Hilton Als, writer, TriBeCa

Taylor Mead, poet, East Soho

Ronnie Eldridge, member of the New York City Council, and
Jimmy Breslin, journalist, Lincoln Center

David Levine, artist, Brooklyn Heights

Melissa Hollbrook Pierson and Luc Sante, writers, Brooklyn

Reverend Al Sharpton, political activist, Brooklyn

Celeste Bartos, and Armand Bartos, architect, Upper East Side

Barbara Jakobson, Upper East Side

Norris Church Mailer, artist, and Norman Mailer, writer,
Brooklyn Heights

John Heilpern, theater critic and writer, West End Avenue

Pierre Bergé, Yves St. Laurent executive, Pierre Hotel

Ed Koch, former New York City mayor, Washington Square

Prince and Princess Alexander Romanoff, Upper East Side

Robert Wilson, director, West Side Highway

Suzanne Farrell, ballet dancer, Upper West Side

John Ashbery, poet, Chelsea

Louise Bourgeois, artist, Chelsea

David Seidner, photographer, East Soho

Jean Vanderbilt, Midtown East Side

Diane von Fürstenberg, fashion designer, Upper East Side

Diane von Fürstenberg, West Village

Charles Rosen, pianist and historian, Upper West Side

Emanuel Dom, model and actor, Midtown West Side

Philip Glass, composer, East Village

Susan Sontag, writer, Chelsea

Cornelia Foss, artist, and Lukas Foss, composer/conductor,
Upper East Side

Olatz Schnabel, model and designer, and Julian Schnabel, painter and
filmmaker, West Village

Alain Coblence, lawyer, Fifth Avenue

Anne H. Bass, patron of the arts, Upper East Side

Helen Carter and Elliott Carter, composer, Greenwich Village

Alexandra Schlesinger, sculptor, and Arthur Schlesinger, Jr., historian,
Beekman Place

Alba Clemente, actress, and Francesco Clemente, artist,
Greenwich Village

Elle McPherson, model and actress, Upper East Side

Nasser Ahari, architect, Upper East Side

Fernando Sanchez, fashion designer, Upper. East Side.

Mario Buatta, interior designer, Upper East Side

Barbara Taylor Bradford, writer, Upper East Side

Richard Meier, architect, Upper East Side

Elizabeth Hardwick, writer, Upper West Side

Gelek, Rinpoche, Midtown East Side

Holly Solomon, art dealer, Midtown East Side

Gita Mehta, writer, and Sonny Mehta, publisher, Upper East Side

Marie Monique Steckel, executive, and Raymond Steckel, lawyer,
Upper West Side

Dennis Oppenheim, artist, TriBeCa

Anthony Haden-Guest, writer and journalist, Upper East Side

Robin Byrd, porn-TV hostess, Fire Island

Roger Prigent, photographer and antiques dealer, Upper East Side

Brooke Hayward, writer, and Peter Duchin, pianist, Murray Hill

Carter Burwell, composer, TriBeCa

Curtis Sliwa, Guardian Angels founder, Chelsea

Mrs. Etienne Boegner, founder of Old Westbury Gardens,
Old Westbury, Long Island

Grace Dudley, Upper East Side

Corice Canton Arman and Arman, artist, TriBeCa

Rita Barros, photographer, Chelsea

Maita di Niscemi, librettist, Upper East Side

Allen Ginsberg, poet, East Village

Barbara Epstein, editor, Upper West Side

Joseph Brodsky, Nobel Laureate poet, Brooklyn Heights

Annette de la Renta and Oscar de la Renta, fashion designer,
Upper East Side

Francoise Gilot, artist and writer, Upper West Side

Francesco Pellizzi, ethnologue and editor, Upper East Side

Marion Wiesel and Elie Wiesel, Nobel Laureate historian, East Side

Joan Didion and John Gregory Dunne, writers, Upper East Side

Konstantin Kakanias, artist, Meat-packing District

Muriel Brandolini, interior decorator, and Nuno Brandolini, merchant banker, Upper East Side

Jean Douglas, artist, and Gordon Douglas, environmentalist,
Upper East Side

Paula Cooper, art dealer, Chelsea

David Garth, political strategist, Upper West Side

Bill Blass, fashion designer, East Side

Henry Buhl, photographer, SoHo

Mary Lumet and Sidney Lumet, filmmaker, Upper West Side

Dominique Nabokov, photographer, Chelsea

The occupants and photo session dates:

Tom Sachs   April 1996
John "Lypsinka" Epperson   September 1995
Nan Goldin   February 1997
Geoffrey Firth   September 1997
Susan Molinari   September 1995
Darryl Turner   September 1995
Ned Rorem   November 1995
Susan Minot   September 1995
Jerome Robbins   September 1995
Tim Lovejoy   September 1995
Leo Lerman and Gray Foy   February 1997
Quentin Crisp   September 1997
Hilton Als   June 1998
Taylor Mead   March 1997
Ronnie Eldridge and Jimmy Breslin   September 1995
David Levine   March 1996
Melissa Hollbrook Pierson and Luc Sante   May 1998
Reverend Al Sharpton   September 1995
Celeste and Armand Bartos   April 1998
Barbara Jakobson   December 1996
Norris Church and Norman Mailer   February 1998
John Heilpern   September 1997
Pierre Bergé   September 1995
Ed Koch   September 1995
Princess and Prince Alexander Romanoff   March 1998
Robert Wilson   September 1995 and April 1997
Suzanne Farrell   February 1997
John Ashbery   September 1995
Louise Bourgeois   February 1997
David Seidner   March 1998
Jean Vanderbilt   March 1998
Diane von Fürstenberg   September 1995 and April 1998
Charles Rosen   March 1997
Emanuel Dom   October 1995
Philip Glass   April 1998
Susan Sontag   September 1995
Cornelia and Lukas Foss   May 1996
Olatz and Julian Schnabel   February 1998
Alain Coblence   September 1995 and November 1997
Anne H. Bass   April 1998
Helen and Elliott Carter   November 1997

Alexandra and Arthur Schlesinger   January 1997

Alba and Francesco Clemente   September 1997

Elle McPherson   September 1997

Nasser Ahari   April 1998

Fernando Sanchez   September 1995

Mario Buatta   September 1995

Richard Meier   April 1998

Barbara Taylor Bradford   October 1997

Elizabeth Hardwick   December 1995

Gelek, Rinpoche   April 1998

Holly Solomon   September 1997

Gita and Sonny Mehta   September 1997

Marie Monique and Raymond Steckel   April 1998

Dennis Oppenheim   September 1995

Anthony Haden-Guest   April 1997

Robin Byrd   September 1995

Roger Prigent   December 1996

Brooke Hayward and Peter Duchin   March 1998

Carter Burwell   May 1998

Curtis Sliwa   September 1995

Mrs.Etienne Boegner   December 1995

Grace Dudley   March 1997

Corice Canton Arman and Arman   September 1995

Rita Barros   October 1995

Maita di Niscemi   May 1998

Allen Ginsberg   September 1995

Barbara Epstein   February 1997

Joseph Brodsky   September 1995

Annette and Oscar de la Renta   March 1997

Francoise Gilot   September 1995

Francesco Pellizzi   September 1997

Marion and Elie Wiesel   September 1995

Joan Didion and John Gregory Dunne   December 1996

Konstantin Kakanias   November 1996

Muriel and Nuno Brandolini   January 1997

Jean and Gordon Douglas   December 1996

Paula Cooper   February 1997

David Garth   September 1995

Bill Blass   April 1998

Henry Buhl   May 1997

Mary and Sidney Lumet   June 1998

Dominique Nabokov   March 1998